Generational Curses And Spiritual Warfare: Spiritual Strategies & Principles Of Victory Against Evil Strongholds

Family spiritual Warfare Books, Volume 3

Johannes Tefo

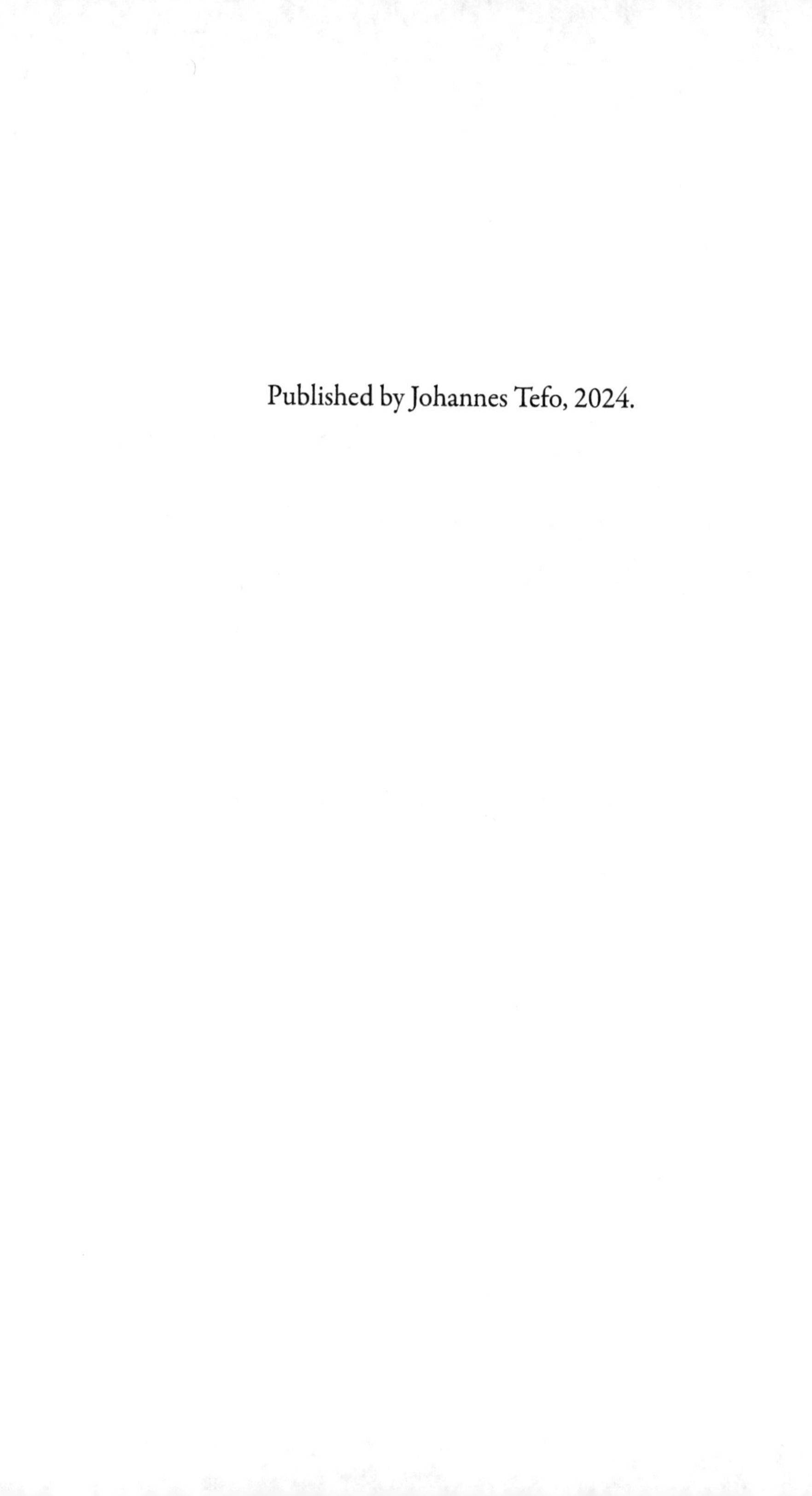

Published by Johannes Tefo, 2024.

Also by Johannes Tefo

Family spiritual Warfare Books
Generational Curses And Spiritual Warfare: Spiritual Strategies &
Principles Of Victory Against Evil Strongholds
Youth's Guide To Spiritual Warfare
A Women's Guide To Spiritual Warfare

Standalone
Deliver Your Soul From Evil
Overcoming Spirit Of Stagnation
The 24: Prophetic Word For This Season 2024 And Beyond
Michael For Warfare
Territorial Spirits: Overcome Evil Strongholds in Your Life And Take
Over Your Community With Strategic Warfare And Winning Prayers
Prayers Against Suicide Spirit
Spiritual Warfare When Enough is Enough
Identity In Christ
Prayers Against Satanic Networks
The Workplace You Need: Spiritual Warfare Prayers That Silence Evil
Powers At Your Workplace.
Deliverance From Mind Control: Be Free And Delivered From Every
Marine Demons Of Mind Control
Times Getting Hard: Scriptures Of Comfort For Hard Days

Battle In The Sea: How To Tackle Spiritual Warfare And Win The Battle

Table of Contents

Dedicated to friends and family in the name of the LORD
GOD.

Stay blessed!

Introduction

When the armies of the LORD came out of Egypt, out of the house of bondage, the joy of the LORD GOD was in their heart. Every man and woman saw the power of the LIVING GOD. Abraham, their father, conversed with the Almighty GOD through dreams and visions. Same as Isaac and Jacob. Here their descendants are, led by fire by night, and clouds by day. The Israelites saw the glory of GOD more than any other generation before or after. It is not a fictional bedtime story; the Exodus did happen.

Moses, the man of GOD, led them out of the house of bondage by the mighty arm of the LORD. They were great in number, imagine more than 600,000 people walking out of the nation of Pharaoh led by one man! All glory to GOD, however, this man Moses, has to be remembered for his strength and courage to stand before kings and queens. An average man cannot do that. An average man cannot reject the benefit of being in the Palace of Pharaoh. Back then, Egypt was the center of the nation. The world wanted a pact with Egypt. Moses rejected all that, for the kingdom of the MOST HIGH.

Moses' story is our story. Be strong and courageous in the LORD! The greatest weapon of every battle is courage. A fearless army is bound to suffer defeat. Courage comes from faith. Bold men can change nations. The world needs the vicar of Moses's leadership. The leadership under the authority of the HOLY SPIRIT. Any power that does not come from the HOLY SPIRIT is destruction at the disposal of a man.

Leadership under the authority of the spirit of GOD brings liberty. Many of us are in bondage. We are living in bondage even though we profess to be redeemed by the mighty hand of the LORD. The nation of Israel was in the wilderness, and when the journey was tough, they wanted to go back to Egypt. Don't go back to Pharaoh. Pharaoh will enslave you, use you, and at some point kill you. It is either GOD or Pharaoh. It is either GOD or Babylon.

Satan was behind the nations that enslaved the children of GOD—the Israelites. Israelites we are called to be the light of the nation. However, they dimmed their light and started mingling with other gods. Deliverance comes from the LORD. Liberty comes from the HOLY SPIRIT. When someone leaves the truth of GOD, Satan, presents himself. The truth of GOD is the glory of GOD. Once you are not under the wings of the eagle of GOD, oppression becomes your middle name.

People of GOD, sin separates us from walking with GOD. CHRIST had to come to redeem us from the spiritual bondage of Satan. You cannot be under bondage when you are under the covering of the MOST HIGH. Yes, trouble will come, but will not shake you.

Psalm 34:19-22 Many are the afflictions of the righteous: but the LORD delivereth him
out of them all.
20 He keepeth all his bones: not one of them is broken.
21 Evil shall slay the wicked: and they that hate the righteous shall be desolate.
22 The LORD redeemeth the soul of his servants: and none of them that trust in him shall be desolate.

The nation of Israel was redeemed because of the covenant GOD had with Abraham. When you have a serious covenant with GOD, your altar will always remind GOD to remember you. The same happened with Noah, the covenant he made with GOD redeemed him out destruction by the flood. We only become powerless when we have broken the covenant with the LIVING KING. The blood of the lamb could only save them while under the house. If any went out of the house, would have suffered the same fate as the Egyptians. The blood of JESUS CHRIST covers you when you are in Him.

In CHRIST we have authority over death. The firstborn of the LORD through Christ shall live. As we are in CHRIST, we take upon his power, glory, and personality. As we grow in the spirit of truth, we will no longer be the children of GOD but the Sons of GOD in authority and power. Glory unto the name of the Lord that redeems us always.

As you journey with me through this special book of deliverance, we shall conquer Pharaoh. We shall overthrow the horses and the riders of the chariots in the name of the LORD.

This is what the Psalmist says *"Some trust in chariots, and some in horses: but we will remember the name of the LORD our God. They are brought down and fallen: but we are risen, and stand upright. Save, LORD: let the king hear us when we call"*.

The believe in the one true GOD is pivotal. The key to victory in all things. Many of our forefathers who walked on this earth, many did not trust the LORD and went on to serve other gods. Today as I was going through Deuteronomy 28, and looking at the patterns of our families and our lives, many of us are living in curse rather than in blessings.

According to Deuteronomy 28, this is the characterizes of the blessed in the LORD.

> You are a head, not a tail.
> You are above the nations.
> No evil plague shall come near your house.
> You shall be a lender, not a borrower.
> You shall smite your enemies.
> Rain shall be the portion of your land.
> You are blessed going out and coming in.
> You are prosperous in the market.
> You are a leader, not a follower.
> Illnesses and sicknesses are far from you.

Here are the characteristics of a cursed life.

> Humiliation
> Poverty
> Sicknesses and diseases.

> Persecuted by their enemies.
> Slavery.
> Oppression.
> Closed heavens.
> Tail not a head.
> Beneath not above.
> Working hard but earning peanuts.
> Always borrowing money.
> Living in lack and debt.
> Living in abnormal fear of the unknown.

Exodus 20:4-6 Thou shalt not make unto thee any graven image, or any likeness of any
thing that is in heaven above, or that is in the earth beneath, or that is in the
water under the earth.
5 Thou shalt not bow down thyself to them, nor serve them: for I the LORD
thy God am a jealous God, visiting the iniquity of the fathers upon the children
unto the third and fourth generation of them that hate me; 6 And shewing mercy
unto thousands of them that love me, and keep my commandments.

When we rebel against the will of GOD, we reap bitter results. JESUS CHRIST became a curse for us on the cross—taking all our infirmities and sickness. When you come to CHRIST, He redeems you—canceling all your debt. But you are still liable to break the generation curses of your forefathers. When the door has been open in your family due to rebellion, cruel and harassing spirits do as they wish. Note, GOD forgives you but the generational curses of your family are still there.

Every believer in CHRIST ought to be delivered. There are ancient spirits of different caliber that cannot be seen with the naked eye that are pulling strings in the background. How do you explain it when someone sleeps well but makes up feeling ill every time? How do you explain the frequent headaches that many are experiencing from time to time? Some things do not need medical attention but deliverance. Some things are straight-up demonic!

Sleep it's a gift from GOD. Millions of people do not sleep at night I tell you. When it gets dark, it gets overwhelming. I for one, was like that. I used to wake up every time feeling like someone was strangling me. For more than 5 years, I made sure that I did not switch off the light at night. And a bottle of water will be by my side all the time. Mind you, I was a Christian at the time.

Many immature believers think that the moment you accept JESUS CHRIST in your life, all your problems with be gone. It is the opposite of that. It is a spiritual fight between the children of the light and the children of the darkness. It is a war. A spiritual war.

However, deliverance is children's bread. JESUS CHRIST brought salvation. Not just salvation but total salvation in all things. It is through the power of the HOLY SPIRIT that we shall be free in the name of the LORD.

Through this book, you are about to embark on the journey of self-deliverance. As I am delivered in the LORD, you shall also be delivered. It is the grace of GOD that does all these things. Rejoice in the LORD. JESUS CHRIST has conquered disease and death through the power of His Word, His blood, and His Holy Name.

Faith, love & Deliverance.

In all things, it all comes down to love. It is because of love that GOD sent CHRIST to die on the cross. It was because of love that CHRIST healed all and delivered all those who were oppressed. The will of GOD is love for all mankind. We suffer when we drift away from the will of GOD. Man has his own will, and GOD has a will for man. If our will contradicts the will of GOD, that's where confusion comes in.

We did not come out of thin air. We were created by a supernatural being. We are spiritual beings. We have the same DNA as GOD because we come from him.

Psalm 100:3 Know ye that the LORD he is God: it is he that hath made us, and not we
ourselves; we are his people, and the sheep of his pasture.

We were made and created out of love. The fact that GOD created us out of nothing, is one of the elements of faith. The first being with unshakable faith is not Adam, Enoch, or Abraham, But ALMIGHTY GOD. He spoke the heavens and earth out of nothing. There were no creatures who were on labor building or patching the sky. The Angels of GOD were rejoicing and singing when GOD was in creation mode.

Psalm 33:7-9By the word of the LORD were the heavens made; and all the host of
them by the breath of his mouth.
7 He gathereth the waters of the sea together as an heap: he layeth up the depth in storehouses.
8 Let all the earth fear the LORD: let all the inhabitants of the world stand
in awe of him.
9 For he spake, and it was done; he commanded, and it stood fast.

This is the same principle that we need as believers to manifest the promises of GOD upon our lives. It is through speaking the promises of GOD in faith. Faith holds all things together. It must be by faith if you are to walk and fellowship with the HOLY SPIRIT. CHRIST is the Word of GOD, when you are quoting, confessing, and declaring the Word, you are releasing the person of CHRIST to miraculously work on your behalf and fulfill what you say. And of course, what you pray for and what you decree should always be in line with the scriptures.

Hebrews 11:1-3 Now faith is the substance of things hoped for, the evidence of things not seen.

2 For by it the elders obtained a good report.

3 Through faith we understand that the worlds were framed by the word of God, so that things which are seen were not made of things which do appear.

Faith will allow us to see the promises of GOD while still on this earth. and also, through faith, we overcome the Evil One. A warrior in CHRIST has to be like David and conquer his enemy while on the journey to the promised land.

Deuteronomy 1:8 Behold, I have set the land before you: go in and possess the land which

the LORD sware unto your fathers, Abraham, Isaac, and Jacob, to give unto

them and to their seed after them.

The promised land is a land of rest. The land of the milk and honey. Where honey flows like a mighty river. This is the place where ALMIGHTY GOD is taking you. Where poverty will be a thing of the past. Where MIGHTY ONE will uphold you in His wings like an eagle and lead you with His righteousness. In His riches and wealth, He adds no sorrow. He gives wealth to those He loves even in their sleep.

Deuteronomy 1:21 Behold, the LORD thy God hath set the land before thee: go up and

possess it, as the LORD God of thy fathers hath said unto thee; fear not, neither

be discouraged.

Be strengthened in the LORD. Trust in the LORD GOD of your salvation, you will never be ashamed. Through faith, we shall do great things for the kingdom. And all the curses that follow us shall be the things of the past. Witchcraft has power but does not have the power of Jacob. You are the children of Israel who conquered wars through faith. Who even contended with the Angel of the presence of the LORD, and won, but through faith in the GOD of Abraham.

Like Joshua, we must be encouraged in our walk of faith. I have also noticed that, if you are not inspired, you will slack off. Inspiration is power. Thus, inspiration from the HOLY SPIRIT is the driving force of the Word we read in the bible. Prophets of old we moved and inspired by the spirit of GOD. Prophets like Elijah and Elisha moved in great power and authority through the power of the mighty spirit of GOD. Our walk is the walk of faith, love, and deliverance.

Deuteronomy 1:38 But Joshua the son of Nun, which standeth before thee, he shall go in thither: encourage him: for he shall cause Israel to inherit it.

Generational curse.

The Lord's curse is on the house of the wicked, but He blesses the home of the righteous (Proverbs 3:33).

There is a blessing for every verse in the Bible that you obey. There is a curse for every verse in the Bible that you disobey. If you obey half of the Bible, you are half blessed and half cursed. Decide to follow the whole Bible, not just a selected part of it.

We are the product of a generation that went before us. We still bear the same DNA. CHRIST had to die so that he could restore the signature of GOD in our blood. The serpentine spirit infiltrated the DNA of Adam and Eve. So to rule them with their demonic agenda.

The same applies to the 200 watchers who fell by sleeping with women in the days of Noah. They messed up the whole plan of God—creating a strange hybrid of beings called Nephilim. I strongly believe that some demons that we are in a constant fight with come from a line of these strange beings. You can connect the dots by studying Genesis 6 and the prophetic book of Enoch.

While CHRIST died from our salvation, he did away with death, stripping away Satan's authority over death and hades. Satan does have power but not authority to do according to his will. We can see this in the story of Job. He had to ask permission (Legal right) before he could wreak havoc in the life of Job.

It is to say, even when CHRIST died for our sins, if there are open doors in our lives due to our forefather's Idol worship, witchcraft practices, bowing to the sun, moon, stars, etc. curses are likely to affect our lives. The death of CHRIST stood against death. When Adam and Eve disobeyed the law, spiritual death was the effect. Separation of man from God. Every sin opens a door for demons to afflict and harass you if the door is open.

If you have sinned in your life, you have opened the door for Satan and his demons to attack you, your family, and your church. Sin is a crack in your armor whether known or unknown to you. You or your ancestors have invited Satan to come into your life and work havoc.

Every demon within a person has a legal right before God to be there. Satan is a legalist and knows his rights before God to send demons into a person. Learn to think of Satan as a lawyer demanding his rights before God. Learn to think of JESUS CHRIST as an advocate, a lawyer, defending our rights before God.

These curses are forms of demonic oppression that can enter family lines through the sins of one's ancestors. The consequences of ancestral sins can be perpetuated nearly indefinitely unless the sin is revoked.

The Lord! the Lord! a God merciful and gracious, slow to anger, and abundant in loving-kindness and truth, keeping mercy and loving-kindness for thousands, forgiving iniquity and transgression and sin, but Who will by no means clear the guilty, visiting the iniquity of the fathers upon the children and the children's children, to the third and fourth generation. (Exodus 34:6-7)

A sin of our ancestors that is affecting us is often referred to as a generational curse. These detrimental and destructive forces can be identified by how they manifest, or show up, in our lives. Some of the signs of generational curses are:

❖ genetic disorders
❖ family traits (drug/alcohol addiction, bad temper)
❖ bad luck that cannot be shaken

Negative, harmful things that happen to each generation of a family are curses. Did your ancestors die at a certain age? Do financial problems pop up for no reason keeping you at a level of poverty as it has for your parents and grandparents? Is there a genetic predisposition for diabetes, heart disease, breast cancer, etc.?

Conditions such as these may have scientific, fact-based explanations, but the truths that come from the Bible reveal the real cause. Truth is always stronger than facts when mixed with faith. These conditions are a curse that may be handed down from one generation to the next. They can be taken care of in the Courts of Heaven.

In my family line, most men died from alcohol poisoning. This is the pattern that I have witnessed in my lineage. And until someone brave enough is willing to stand on the gap of priesthood, the pattern is still going to continue.

A generational curse is the legalistic means by which the demonic realm acquires a family line. The curse consists of the unrepented sin of our ancestors. It travels down the family line—but can be broken through the blood of Jesus Christ!

Things don't just happen. They do happen for a reason. A curse without a cause is useless. It has to have the roots, and that would be its legal right to stand on. Earlier on, I knew that something was up, whenever the opportunity arises, be it a job or something related to career advancement, the night before the interview I will sleep with a woman in my dream.

And I will wake up frustrated and feeling messy. I later realized that this was the destroying spirit at the edge of my breakthrough in the form of spiritual women—some call it incubus. Through personal revelation and study, I realized that this was a familiar demon in my family, and the root of it comes from my forefathers' idol worship.

They made a pact with water spirits for witchcraft powers, and prosperity, especially in agriculture. Even though I was a born-again believer, some nights I used to struggle with this thing. I would like to put it this way, some curses come from GOD, as written in Deuteronomy 28, some curses from witches and wizards, and some curses from yourself by speaking down on yourself, not according to what the scriptures say about you.

Bad Luck Clings to You

You will be cursed in the city and cursed in the field...You will be cursed when you come in and you will be cursed when you go out. (Deuteronomy 28:16 & 19)

Does bad luck seem to follow you around? Do unfortunate situations seem to happen over and over no matter where you go or what you do? This may be a curse or a test from God. Bad luck just includes a bunch of bad things not working out such as relationships, marriage, career, finance, and health. It was strange in my home that we would go to sleep and tomorrow someone would wake up feeling ill. We thought it was just normal. There is nothing normal when demons are involved.

It is depressing and heartbreaking to see someone spend more than 10 years of his or her life jobless. This is the kind of environment we grew up in. Not that we are obsessive about the spiritual aspect of things, however, by studying the patterns, you can see that the dark powers are hovering over the territory.

Bad luck comes from the Devil. He is the orchestrator of evil things through his demons and human agents. Millions of human agents work in the kingdom of darkness. In particular, in the marine kingdom—underwater realm. These agents are mainly concerned with breaking marriage, relationships, friendships, business etc. And making sure that their victims stand no chance of achieving in life.

Only the power of GOD can deliver you from the powers of the enemy.

You shall carry much seed out into the field and shall gather little in, for the locust shall consume it. (Deuteronomy 28:38)

"Carrying seed out" means you are working and getting little back for it. Toiling for our food was the result of the first curse God spoke of when Adam and Eve fell. He reiterates it here. If no amount of hard work gets you ahead, this could be due to a curse that has been passed down from your ancestors.

Bad Relationships

You shall betroth a wife, but another man shall lie with her...
(Deuteronomy 28:30)

Unfaithfulness in a marriage causes a generational curse to form. Does it seem like you marry the wrong person time after time? God can change hearts and make any relationship work if given the chance. We have free will, but if you clear generational curses in the Courts of Heaven, you won't be fighting an uphill battle.

Another wonder that I have seen is polygamy at play. In some families, it is a pattern. It started with Grand Grand Pa leading to your generation. In many south African cultures, especially in chieftaincy families, this is the norm.

Many justify polygamy in the case of Abraham. It was not GOD who told Abraham to have three wives. Abraham's primary wife was Sarah. It was Sarah's idea to conceive through Hagar. Ishmael was born through Hagar. Then After Sarai died, Abraham took another wife. It is understandable and scriptural to take another wife when your primary one has died.

Even in the case of Jacob. It was a norm in those times to take a second wife when your first wife did not conceive. Polygamy was not part of GOD's plan. Marriage is a union between a man and a woman.

If it is not from GOD, then it is from the enemy. Within the structure of polygamy, there is misery, depression, and lonely individuals who are neglected and less valued than the other partner. It is a chaos of women competing with each other to earn their partner's favor. We can see this in the lives of Rebecca and Leah, Sarah and Hagar, Hannah and Peninnah, and many more in the bible.

In today's culture, especially in Zulu culture, there is still that spirit of polygamy. You will hear them saying "my father had 3 wives, I gotta have 3 wives too". The thing is, even if financially the brother is not at the point of taking 3 wives, he will continue. It is a generational curse without a doubt. However, it may not seem like it. But it is!

While I was in a certain Pentecostal church, those African-initiated ones, I used to receive prophecies that I was going to marry five wives. That I come from a linage of king, that, GOD is going to bless me with five wives. To tell you the truth, it did sit well with me. I cannot even image myself with that hard work.

I now know that the brother was not lying but telling what he was seeing. It's a pattern that has to be broken, not cherished. The law of Moses said the king has to be the man of one wife. King Solomon and kings after him broke the law of Moses.

Breaking curses.

The Lord's curse is on the house of the wicked, but He blesses
the home of the righteous (Proverbs 3:33).

Confession of sin.

In the first year of Darius the son of Ahasuerus, of the seed of the Medes,
which was made king over the realm of the Chaldeans;
2 In the first year of his reign I Daniel understood by books the number of
the years, whereof the word of the LORD came to Jeremiah the prophet,
that he
would accomplish seventy years in the desolations of Jerusalem.
3 And I set my face unto the Lord God, to seek by prayer and supplications,
with fasting, and sackcloth, and ashes:
4 And I prayed unto the LORD my God, and made my confession, and
said,
O Lord, the great and dreadful God, keeping the covenant and mercy to
them
that love him, and to them that keep his commandments; 5 We have
sinned, and
have committed iniquity, and have done wickedly, and have rebelled, even
by
departing from thy precepts and from thy judgments:
6 Neither have we hearkened unto thy servants the prophets, which spake
in

thy name to our kings, our princes, and our fathers, and to all the people of the

land.

I cannot write the whole prayer of Daniel but through this passage, there is so much wisdom we can learn as the body of CHRIST concerning the confession of sin. It was after Daniel understood the book of Prophet Jeremiah that he started to make bold moves. After this, Daniel has never been the same.

First and foremost, the Word of GOD is paramount to your redemption. Daniel would have not prayed if he hadn't read from the book of Jeremiah. The second thing is the understanding of the Word. Until you understand the scripture, you will still be on the same level.

We should study the Word of GOD with understanding. And understanding comes from the HOLY SPIRIT. Allow your understanding to overshadow the works of the HOLY SPIRIT.

The third principle of deliverance we can look at is prayer and fasting. The prayer of a righteous man of faith will always amount to great things. Daniel changed the history of his people. He is still relevant today to study his work, like Enoch, Daniel also saw the long-awaited Messiah, JESUS CHRIST in a vision 1000 years ago before the time.

The mysteries of the kingdom of GOD, the prophetic future, and the end, are wrapped in Daniel' and John's visions and revelations. In the whole land of Babylon, there was no man of Daniel caliber. Yet humble in spirit that he attributed everything to the glory of GOD. He was not moved by gifts like the prophets we have today. Our generation is a prophet for profit.

As we look at the third principle, fasting, and prayer, this is where Daniel set his face unto the LORD with heartfelt prayers. He did not only prayer for himself but for the whole nation. In humility, he said, "I and the people have sinned". This is the kind of prayer GOD will not despise. Prayers that yield fruit.

Primarily, the purpose of fasting is self-humbling. It is a scriptural means ordained by God for us to humble ourselves before Him. Throughout the Bible, God requires His people to humble themselves before Him. Many different passages of Scripture emphasize this.

The primary purpose for fasting, as revealed in the Bible, is self-humbling. Fasting is a scriptural way to humble ourselves. All through the Bible God required His people to humble themselves before Him. God has revealed that a simple, practical way to humble ourselves is through fasting.

And it was an answered prayer in the case of Daniel. Even though he had to contend with principalities and powers of darkness of Babylon.

The word of GOD causes us to examine our hearts and repent. It is all about aligning your heart with the mind of GOD. A way to look at it is to study the 10 commandments and look at where you and your family are to GOD. Some things don't need you to be super spiritual but to be observant—to look at the pattern within your lineage as we are dealing with generation curses.

And confess every sin as you come in light with CHRIST. CHRIST is the light of the glory of GOD. In glory, there is no darkness. GOD dwells in high mighty glory on high.

1 John 1:8 If we say that we have no sin, we deceive ourselves, and the truth is not in

us.

1 John 1:9 If we confess our sins, he is faithful and just to forgive us our sins, and to

cleanse us from all unrighteousness.

1 John 1:7 But if we walk in the light, as he is in the light, we have fellowship one

with another, and the blood of Jesus Christ his Son cleanseth us from all sin.

It doesn't matter the weight of the sin. There is no big or light sin, every type of sin can get you to hell place. The only different there would be the amount of punishment your soul will get. I do not want to dwell much on this, but folks, there is a place called hell. And it is written that only the pure in heart shall see the face of GOD. Holiness is still a matter of today as it was in ancient times. This is the type of preaching that the church of CHRIST avoids.

Confession of sin means you are no longer going to revert to do the same thing. Repentance is the change of heart and mind. The HOLY SPIRIT will help our weak flesh to overcome temptations. Faith must be above it all. Faith holds the house together. The power is in your mouth. The tongue is your asset in this kingdom business.

The more Word you hear, the more faith you will walk in.

James 5:16, "Confess your faults one to another, and pray one for another, that ye may be healed . The effectual fervent prayer of a righteous man availeth much."

Romans 10:9-11 That if thou shalt confess with thy mouth the Lord Jesus, and shalt believe
in thine heart that God hath raised him from the dead, thou shalt be saved.
10 For with the heart man believeth unto righteousness; and with the mouth
confession is made unto salvation.
11 For the scripture saith, Whosoever believeth on him shall not be ashamed.

Salvation prayer.

Father in JESUS Christ Name, I believe He died on the cross for my sins and rose again from the dead. I am redeemed His blood and I belong to you, and I want to live for you. I confess all my sins—known and unknown—
I'm sorry for them all. I renounce them all. I forgive all others as I want you to forgive me. Forgive me now and cleanse me with your blood. I thank

*you for the blood of JESUS Christ which cleanses me now from all sin.
And I come to you now as my deliverer. You know my special needs—the
thing that binds, that torments, that defiles; that evil spirit, that unclean
spirit—I claim the promise of your word, "Whosoever that calleth on the
name of the Lord shall be DELIVERED." I call upon you now. In the
name
of the Lord JESUS Christ, deliver me and set me free. Satan, I renounce
you and all your works. I loose myself from you, in the name of JESUS,
and I command you to leave me right now in JESUS' name. Amen!"*

Holy spirit prayer.

*Heavenly Father, I thank You that You love me.
I thank You for every blessing You have bestowed upon my family
and me.
I believe Jesus died on the cross to take away the sins of the
world.
Today I ask for the gift of the baptism of the Holy Spirit.
Jesus said, "If anyone is thirsty, let him come to Me and drink"
(John 7:37).
My Father in Heaven, I am very thirsty and I have come to
drink!
I believe in the Father; the Son, Jesus; and the Holy Spirit.
Let the streams of living water flow through me.
Let my spirit pray to You, Father.
Let my spirit sing to You, Father.
Let my tongue utter mysteries.
Let the gifts I receive build me up and build up Your Church.
I praise You, Father, and I worship You with all my heart.
I seek You, Father. Take my hand and bring me deeper into You
each day.
I receive the gift of baptism of the Holy Spirit in faith.*

I thank You for it.
In Jesus' name, I pray. Amen.

Renouncing Prayers.

Forgiveness Prayer

Heavenly Father, thank You for sending Your Son, Jesus Christ,
to defeat the works of the devil.
Jesus, I thank You for what You did for me on the cross. I know
You died for the deepest darkest part of me. You have come to
bring me eternal life, and it is that life that I want in the fullest.
I invite Your light into my darkness.

Self-Hatred

"For You created my inmost being; You knit me together in my
mother's womb" (Psalm 139:13).
Please forgive me for hating myself, for hating my body, for wanting
to hurt myself, and for wanting to die.
"I praise You because I am fearfully and wonderfully made; Your
works are wonderful, I know that full well" (Psalm 139:14).

Family

Please forgive me for harboring anger and resentment toward
any members of my family. I choose to forgive them today.
I forgive my parents, siblings, and other relatives for their abusive
actions.
I forgive my parents for rejecting me and for physically or emotionally
abandoning me.
I forgive the members of my family who sexually abused me,
manipulated me, or who spoke curses over me.
I choose to honor and bless my father and mother.
I break the curse of divorce in my family line. Any curse on my
family, known or unknown, is broken from this day forward,
in Jesus' name.

Anger

Forgive me for my thoughts of anger, temper, and fits of rage.

Forgive me for my prejudices, bitterness, and resentment.
Forgive me for blaspheming Your name; forgive me for my
pride.
Forgive me for emotionally tearing down women with my words
or for harboring hatred toward men.
I want to step out of this emotional darkness and into Your
light.

Occult/Idolatry/Witchcraft

Forgive me for my involvement in witchcraft, the occult, and
any blood covenants I have made.
Forgive me for consulting with psychics, palm readers, and
Tarot card readers; forgive me for seeking supernatural powers
that are not from You.
Forgive me for talking to the dead and channeling. I break all
ties to the enemy now.
I renounce all pacts made with satan by my ancestors or myself.
I choose to bless all those in my lineage and my new life in You,
from this day forward.

Sexual Immorality/Adultery

Forgive me for having sex outside of marriage.
Forgive me for the rape(s) I have committed.
Forgive me for blaming myself for being raped or molested as a
child.
Forgive me for the self-hatred and anger I have bottled up from
being sexually abused.
Forgive me for my fornication, adultery, and for feeding my feelings
of lust. Forgive my pornography, sexual perversions, group
sex, and sexual obsessions.
Forgive me for homosexuality or lesbianism.
Forgive me for participating in sexual acts and rituals of the
occult.
Forgive my family for their ungodly participation in sexual sin

and for any act(s) of incest.
Jesus, please bless me, forgive me, and wash me clean from sexual immorality.

Untimely Death

Forgive me, God, for being angry with You for the untimely death of my child, spouse, parents, siblings, or loved one(s).

Forgive me, God, for blaming You for giving my loved one a terminal illness. I recognize that sickness, death, and disease are the works of satan. They are not from You.

Forgive me for having an abortion.

Forgive me for having paid for, suggested, or forced a woman to have an abortion.

Father, heal my unresolved grief. Forgive me and my family for any curse of death that may be upon us. Bless us with life, in Jesus' name.

Religious

Forgive me for relying on works by following religious doctrines and legalisms, rather than Your grace for my salvation.

Forgive me for participating in spiritual oaths, vows, and rituals in a church that preached a false doctrine of Jesus Christ.

Forgive my family for participating in these legalisms and false doctrines. I wish to live under the covenant of the Gospel of Jesus Christ. Bless my family from this moment forward.

Sickness/Illness

Forgive me for believing the lie that, in my sickness, I was suffering for You.

Jesus, You came to destroy the works of the devil. These include sickness, death, and disease.

Father, please release my family from the curse of hereditary illness. I break all curses of sickness and disease off my family and me, in Jesus' name.

Addiction

Forgive me for my addiction(s) to alcohol, cigarettes, drugs, gluttony, pornography, (name of other addiction).
Forgive me for allowing my addictions to destroy my family.
Release my family and me from the curse and bondage of addiction, in Jesus' name.

Prayer of Repentance

Father, forgive me for blaming You, for blaming myself, and for blaming others.
I believe, receive, and request Your grace, mercy, forgiveness, and covering now. Release me from any curse as I receive Your freedom. Thank You for Your blessings and favor in my life.
Amen.

Warfare Warrior scriptures.

Gen. 1:28 - We are to subdue the earth.

Gen. 3:15 - JESUS bruised the head of Satan.

Ex. 15:3 - The Lord is a man of war: the Lord is his name.

Num. 23:8 - How shall I curse, whom God hath not cursed?

Psa. 5:10 - Let them fall by their own counsels.

Psa. 6:10 - Let all mine enemies be ashamed and sore vexed.

Psa. 7:15 - And is fallen in the ditch which he made.

Psa. 8:6 - Thou madest him to have dominion over the works of thy hands.

Psa. 10:15 - Break thou the arm of the wicked and evil men.

Psa. 17:13 - Arise , O Lord, disappoint him, cast him down.

Psa. 24:8 - The Lord mighty in battle.

Psa. 28:4 - Render to them their desert.

Psa. 35:8 - Let his net that he hath hid catch himself.

Psa. 37:14 - And to slay such as be of upright conversation.

Psa. 55:9 - Destroy, O Lord, and divide their TONGUES.

Psa. 57:6 - Into the midst whereof they are fallen themselves.

Psa. 58:6 - Break their teeth, O God, in their mouth.

Psa. 59:11 - Scatter them by thy power; and bring them down.

Psa. 68:18 - Thou hast led captivity captive.

Psa. 69:22 - Which should have been for their welfare, let it become a trap.

Psa. 83:9 - A prayer against them that oppress the church.

Psa. 109:17 - As he loved cursing, so let it come unto him.

Psa. 109:28 - When they arise, let them be ashamed.

Psa. 109:29 - Let them cover themselves with their own confusion.

Psa. 140:9 - Let the mischief of their own lips cover them.

Psa. 149:6-9 - A two edged sword in their hand.

Prov. 26:2 - So the curse causeless shall not come.

Isa. 53:12 - He shall divide the spoil with the strong.

Isa. 54:17 - Every tongue arising against thee in judgment thou shalt condemn.

Isa. 58:6 - Fast - Loose - Undo - Free - Break

Jer. 1:10 - Set - Root - Pull - Destroy - Throw - Build - Plant

Jer. 48:10 - Cursed be he that keepeth back his sword from blood.

Jer. 51:20 - Thou art my battle axe and weapons of war.

Matt. 5:44 - Love your enemies.

Matt. 10:7-8 - Preach - Heal - Cleanse - Raise - Cast - Give

Matt. 12:29 - We are to bind the strong man, Satan, and spoil his house.

Matt. 18:18-19 - Bind - Loose - Agree

Matt. 28:20 - Teaching to observe all things whatsoever I have commanded you.

Luke 4:18 - Preach / Heal / Deliver / Sight / Liberty

Luke 8:1 - We should do the works of God in every city and village.

Luke 10:18 - Satan is a defeated foe.

Luke 10:19 - God gave us power over all the power of the enemy.

Luke 11:22 - We are stronger than Satan through JESUS CHRIST.

John 12:31 - Now shall the prince of this world be cast out.

John 16:11 - The prince of this world has been judged by JESUS.

Rom. 16:20 - And the God of peace shall bruise Satan under your feet shortly.

I Cor. 4:12 - Being reviled we bless; being persecuted we suffer it.

II Cor. 10:4 - We are to pull down the strongholds of Satan.

Eph. 3:10 - The church is to make its presence known to the principalities.

Eph. 6:12 - We wrestle not against flesh and blood but against evil forces.

Eph. 6:16 - Ye shall be able to quench all the fiery darts of the wicked.

Col. 2:15 - JESUS spoiled principalities and powers.

II Tim. 1:10 - Our Savior JESUS CHRIST who hath abolished death.

II Tim. 2:26 - Help others recover themselves out of the snare of the Devil.

Heb. 2:8 - Thou hast put all things in subjection under his feet.

Heb. 2:14 - He might destroy him that had the power over death.

James 4:7 - Resist the Devil and he will flee from you.

I John 3:8 - Son of God was manifested to destroy the works of the Devil.

I John 5:5 - We are overcomers because we believe in JESUS, the Son of God.

Rev. 12:11 - Overcome by blood of Lamb, word of testimony and love not lives.

Rev. 12:17 - We are at war with the forces of evil.

Pleading the blood of Jesus.

Under the Law, almost everything is purified using blood, and without the shedding of blood, there is neither release from sin and its guilt nor the remission of the due and merited punishment for sins. (Hebrews 9:22).

The blood of JESUS is life. In His blood, there is the spirit of life. The spirit of life that overpowers death. Death is no longer prideful because CHRIST has destroyed its power. Many do not realize that death is a personality, death is a spirit.

When GOD of Israel was bringing Israel out of Egypt, at the last plague, he sent the angel of death to kill every firstborn of Egypt. This is not just an ordinary angel that you can encounter at any time, it is a pale angel that resembles the place of the dead itself. It is a fallen angel.

He sends them evil angels to destroy them.
Isaiah 45:7 I form the light, and create darkness: I make peace, and create
evil: I the
LORD do all these things.

Death is your enemy. Darkness is your enemy. We are to walk in the light of GOD. And the light of GOD is accepting the power of the blood of JESUS to cleanse you and redeem you out of the hand of the Evil One. For a long time, the enemy has been playing chess with our lives.

The HOLY SPIRIT is the remedy for all the chaos that is in this world. When we are empowered by the power of the blood of the lamb and by the mighty spirit of GOD, we shall arise and shine—and be the beacon of light upon this earth.

Isaiah 61:31 Arise, shine; for thy light is come, and the glory of the LORD
is risen
upon thee.
2 For, behold, the darkness shall cover the earth, and gross darkness the
people: but the LORD shall arise upon thee, and his glory shall be seen
upon

3 And the Gentiles shall come to thy light, and kings to the brightness of thy rising.

The death of JESUS CHRIST brought light upon the darkness. He brought the truth to the lie that has been ongoing since the early days of the earth. He shed his precious blood for every nation, not just the people of his time, but even generations to come shall be justified by the power of the work of the cross.

The blood of CHRIST is enough. Even if we can kill all the animals of this world, none can equate to the blood of the sinless lamb.

You do not have to supplement the work of CHRIST with your self-righteousness. CHRIST himself is your righteousness, your light, your glory, and your salvation indeed. Open your heart to the truth of the gospel, simple faith can get you going.

My testimony about the power of the blood!

The blood of Jesus has power. Every family of the Israelites during the Passover, were delivered from death by the blood of the lamb upon their doorsteps. The blood delivers us from the one who is called death. You cannot be in destruction if you leave this world covered by the blood of the lamb.

Those who are covered by the blood of the lamb are overcomers. They have overcome the world and the evil one. The evil one is the god of this world. The prince, Satan. It is through the power of the blood of Jesus that we stand in confidence and can defeat the enemy. If it wasn't the blood, we would have long ago faded and destroyed. In the DNA of the blood of CHRIST is the mighty spirit of the LIVING GOD.

I have witnessed great deliverance in my life for just singing the hymns about the power of the blood of Jesus.

Psalm 118:14-15 The LORD is my strength and song, and is become my salvation.

The voice of rejoicing and salvation is in the tabernacles of the righteous

The blood still has the power to deliver you from idol worship, witchcraft, and marine powers. In the spirit realm, the blood of CHRIST is the greatest light that the Devil and his demons cannot stand.

A believer in spirit who is covered by the blood is glorious with the mighty light of GOD. Only when the light is dimmed by sin, the enemy and demons can attack. The LORD JESUS once opened my spiritual eyes to see the science behind the blood when believers plead it and apply it to their lives.

JESUS CHRIST is light and whoever comes to his house is in the house of light. We should walk in authority, not just talk about it, but walk in it. Most of the time, the church talks about power and authority but it is only a fraction of believers out of billions of Christians who walk in power. Already there is an outpouring of the HOLY SPIRIT. The HOLY SPIRIT is yearning for fellowship but we just ignoring it.

I remember at one point I was singing a well-known gospel song and I heard the voice of the HOLY SPIRIT saying "Sing unto me your own song". Every one of us has a song of deliverance. You wonder sometimes waking up humming a song you don't even know, my friend, it is the work of the HOLY SPIRIT. Sometimes you just recall a scripture, or the scripture just pops up in your mind for no reason, it is the scripture for your deliverance for that moment.

It is truly vital to guard against our minds and transform our minds through scripture meditation. GOD uses your mind more than dreams and visions. Some thoughts are from the enemy. Some thoughts are from you. And some thoughts are from GOD. The discerning spirit will help you to know which is which. It shouldn't be the lost art in the body of CHRIST—the Spirit of discernment.

As we are dealing with generational curses and spiritual warfare, you will realize that sweet prayers sometimes do not yield fruits. There is a time for everything under the sun. when you are dealing with powerful forces, it is time for war. We know we a victorious because He who is in us is greater than He who is in the world. Indeed, the prince of this world has much influence since many are not for us but against us—but in the name of the LORD we shall conquer.

A life of spirit is when you are dead in CHRIST. When your flesh is dead in CHRIST you arise and live a life that is pleasing to the father. Many who have experienced greater glory in this kingdom are those who sacrificed their flesh. Who upheld the principle of faith. And the power that comes through the Word. When you magnify the Word, you honor the LORD himself.

And you, being dead in your sins and the uncircumcision of your flesh, hath he quickened together with him, having forgiven you all trespasses; Blotting out the handwriting of ordinances that was against us, which was contrary to us, and took it out of the way, nailing it to his cross; And having spoiled principalities and powers, he made a shew of them openly, triumphing over them in it. (Colossians 2:14).

Jesus provided the payment necessary for our sins. "Pleading the blood" is a legal term for stating a reason for your innocence. You are stating that because of the blood of Jesus, this sin is removed from you, blotted out, and it is remembered no more. Imagine Satan's frustration: He keeps putting charges against us and when we plead the blood his evidence just disappears.

But as it now is, He has once for all at the consummation and close of the ages appeared to put away and abolish sin by His sacrifice [of Himself].
(Hebrews 9:26)

This is our high priest forever. The priest after the order of Melchizedek. Not ordained by man but above. The bread that comes from above that tumbles the table of sin. This is JESUS CHRIST THE SON OF THE LIVING GOD.

COME TO THE WELL OF LIVING WATER. Your life will never be the same. In prayer, especially heartfelt prayers, sincere worship, and praise. In Him, we have redemption in all things. Brothers and sisters, keep the fire of your prayer altar burning. Time is too short. We are definitely not in the last days but last hour.

In Him we have redemption through His blood, the forgiveness of our trespasses, (Ephesians

1:7 ESV)

The Secret is in the blood

When dealing with the principalities and powers, the secret is in the blood. The power of the blood of Jesus is still as effective as it was 2000 years ago. Hebrews 13:8 'Jesus is the same yesterday, today and forever'. Tapping into the power of God is tapping into the power of the blood of Jesus Christ.

We overcome the enemy through the blood of Jesus. We are only made perfect through the blood of Jesus. When we say Jesus spoiled the principalities, powers, and rulers of the darkness, we mean the death of the cross. When the blood of Yashua touched the ground, God reconciled all things unto Him, and victory was won. It comes from nothing but the blood of Jesus.

The power of a Christian life is in the blood of Jesus Christ. Apostle Paul says, that without the shedding of the blood, there is no remission of sins. Cover the atmosphere with the blood of Jesus, your city, town, village, etc. We wage war with spiritual beings in the high places. You cannot win the fight if you don't engage the enemy in your city. Binding the city will help you to expel the lesser demons in your household, marriage, church, and your personal life.

Our souls are atoned by the blood. It is the blood that brought deliverance to our forefathers in the days of Moses. The Lord's Passover rests on the sacrificial blood of the lamb as the protector and refuge against the destroyer of the firstborn in Egypt. Every Christian who comes to the presence of God comes boldly by the blood of Christ. It is the blood of Christ that brings all people near to God.

Behind the blood, there is a mystery. I can tell you that, when you call upon the blood of the precious Lord, you call upon the very presence of the life of GOD.

Leviticus 17:11 For the life of the flesh is in the blood: and I have given it to you upon the altar to make an atonement for your souls: for it is the blood that maketh an atonement for the soul.

Revelation 12:11 And they overcame him by the blood of the Lamb, and by the word of their testimony; and they loved not their lives unto the death.

Ephesians 1:7 In whom we have redemption through his blood, the forgiveness of sins, according to the riches of his grace;

Pleading the Blood of Jesus through prayers is the most effective way of destroying the works of the enemy. The Blood of Jesus means life and the blood contains fresh power of God. It is that same blood that speaks better things than the blood of Abel. This is the redemptive power plan of God for mankind.

When you plead the blood of Jesus in prayers, you are exercising the power of God that is in the blood.

Leviticus 17:11 For the life of the flesh is in the blood: and I have given it to you upon the altar to make an atonement for your souls: for it is the blood that maketh an atonement for the soul.

There are great testimonies from people using the blood of Jesus to wage serious war against their enemies and God fought for them. Pleading the blood of Jesus shows that you are applying the blood to your life and situations just like the Israelites applied the blood of the lamb to their doorposts and were protected from destruction and attacks (Exodus 12).

The power in the blood of Jesus is powerful to save, heal, and deliver. The spiritual meaning of the blood of Jesus means forgiveness of our sins. The Bible says Jesus shed His blood on the cross of Calvary. That precious blood stands for our salvation. No other powers can contest that unique blood of Jesus. God has made provision for the blood as a weapon for war and protection.

Pleading the Blood of Jesus is a legal term that means to stand on the spiritual rights that are "legally" ours through the Blood that Jesus shed for the forgiveness of our sins. The Blood of Jesus gives us rights over the devil and rights with God because God honors the Blood of His Son.

Watch your words!

You will be judged according to your words. And you will be justified according to your words. Words have power. It is the Word that created the earth and the heaven we see. JESUS CHRIST walked in power and authority because of the word of power was in His mouth. The kingdom of GOD is the kingdom of the demonstration of the power of the Word of GOD.

Paul and Peter used the same principle of the power of words to accomplish their ministry mission. We as the body of CHRIST should realize how powerful words are. In the kingdom of darkness, they know the power of words, that no magic or cure can take place without the words.

However, words are empowered by spirits. It is either the HOLY SPIRIT or demons from the realm of darkness. We ought to be cation of what we say, and what we speak about ourselves. Many have cursed themselves without their knowledge, and the Devil held them accountable with their words. It serves the enemy with the power of legal right when the believers use words negatively over their lives and over the lives of others.

Proverb 18:20 A man's belly shall be satisfied with the fruit of his mouth;
and with the
increase of his lips shall he be filled.

This scripture still touches upon the power of your words. Your words have an impact on this world and you cannot take back when you have already spoken. That is why CHRIST spoke that a man shall be condemned or justified by the words of his mouth. With your words, you can curse or bless.

As you speak and believe, it shall be. When inspired by the spirit of GOD, you can speak life to the dead situation.

Proverbs 18:21 Death and life are in the power of the tongue: and they that love it shall

eat the fruit thereof.

By now we know that Satan is a legalist. He holds everyone accountable also for their words. Some words can be snared. For instance, when you always think of yourself as nobody, as amounting to nothing in life, low confidence, and a negative outlook in life would give the enemy access to mess with you more.

Demons love to harass. And they hate Christians. Which means they hate you. And as much as they hate you, they want to possess you. Our lives are negotiated day and night by the enemy but through the grace of the LORD, we are still standing. There is power in the name of JESUS. His blood is still interceding for us before the mighty FATHER!

Therefore, increase the fruit of your lips to speak blessings in your life and the life of others. Speak the will and the mind of CHRIST. In CHRIST we win. In CHRIST we are conquerors. CHRIST is the lion. The righteous are bold like lions. Generational curses shall be a thing of the past. CHRIST became a curse so that we can be blessed. In the name of the LORD be blessed!

Confess scripture to your situation. Proclaim who you are in CHRIST. See yourself how CHRIST sees you. A new fresh perspective shall arise in you!

Psalm 92:10 But my horn shalt thou exalt like the horn of an unicorn: I shall be

anointed with fresh oil.

Blessed life of walking in the ways of GOD.

The sad note is that; our forefathers did not walk in the ways of the LORD faithfully. We know that the foundation of the throne of GOD is holiness and righteousness. If you are to walk with GOD, there is no negotiation—Holiness and righteousness are a must.

We know the pattern of the ark Moses was commanded to be built. GOD seats upon the mercy seat. Mercy and grace rule over law. Thus, He does not punish us according to our transgression. He is the merciful GOD. However, His principles still apply. His Word does not change. Sin is a sin. And sin produces evil results.

Men and women are commanded to walk in the commandments of GOD. Men and women were called to magnify the law—and uphold righteousness. However, chose their own will of fleshly desires. GOD does not curse but the law works against you when you transgress it. and through my observation, rebellion has always been that one sin that separated men away from GOD.

Isaiah 1:4 Ah sinful nation, a people laden with iniquity, a seed of evildoers,

children that are corrupters: they have forsaken the LORD, they have provoked

the Holy One of Israel unto anger, they are gone away backward.

The spirit of rebellion will cause you to forsake the LORD. Rebellion is the same as witchcraft. It is like you know what right thing to do but opt to do your own thing—moved by your self-centered desires just like King Saul.

We are called by the blessed One who has blessed us with all spiritual blessings in the heavenly places. Everything in this life starts in the spirit realm before it can manifest physically. Just for a second look at how witchcraft operates, witches and wizards Astra project into people's homes to speak evil incantations and bind curses over individuals. Upon waking, you will realize that something is not right.

As someone who grew up in villages in South Africa, I have seen the first-hand eye of the power of witchcraft curses upon the lives of individuals. It is foolish to deny that Satan has no power. JESUS CHRIST empowered His Apostle before he sent them. It was necessary because of the two powers that clashes—the power of the kingdom of light and the kingdom of darkness.

All powers come from GOD. However, the Devil uses his power for destruction. Life is spiritual. And life comes from spirit. therefore, allow me to say, that, blessings are spiritual. Wealth is spiritual. Money is spiritual. You may see money as a valuable paper but there is spirit behind money. Approach life from the spiritual standpoint, you shall see things differently.

Apostle Paul says "For though we walk in the flesh, we do not war after the flesh:(For the weapons of our warfare are not carnal, but mighty through God to the pulling down of strong holds;)".

A bloody war we will not fight but a spiritual one with the powers of evil. It is through GOD that we stand a chance against our enemy—Satan. It is through the spirit of GOD that testifies within us that we are the children of GOD. The Sons and daughters of the MOST HIGH who walk in spirit and truth of the gospel of CHRIST.

Righteousness produces a blessed life. The upright shall inherit the kingdom of GOD. The kingdom of GOD includes everything, even a life of financial success. It is not the will of GOD for man to suffer in poverty and lack. It has been ingrained in the minds of many believers that if you are poor, you are living it for GOD.

It all comes down to spiritual maturity. You can be wealthy and still keep GOD first. There is no glory in lack. The advancement of the kingdom of GOD goes forward when there are pure kingdom financers with GOD's intentions. The level of grace in one's life can determine how far he can go with the LORD.

Be blessed so that you can be a blessing to others just like Abraham. In many cases, lack, stagnation, non-achievement in life, and poverty, are the result of someone living in the curse. As you read Deuteronomy 28, blessings or curses, you realize that a cursed life is the result of disobedience to the will of GOD. While a blessed life is an act of faith and obedience.

We will look at the blessed life. And a contrast of the cursed life.

You shall be above nations.
1 And it shall come to pass, if thou shalt hearken diligently unto the voice of the LORD thy God, to observe and to do all his commandments which I command thee this day, that the LORD thy God will set thee on high above all
nations of the earth:

The blessed in the LORD are above others in different areas of life. It does not mean they do not encounter challenges but the LORD GOD is their refuge in times of trouble. The upright in the LORD are the inheritors of the kingdom of GOD. If you diligently obey the voice of the LORD, He shall talk to you about opportunities of greater glory where His hand is, the choice of who to marry, career, finances, etc. the LORD shall manifest in glory in your life.

Elijah prospered because he mastered the listening skills of the small still voice of the ALMIGHTY, imagine if he had not caught in spirit what the move of the spirit was at that time. Imagine if he was not available at a certain time for the ravens to bring him food. Obedience to the voice of GOD is your treasure to your wealth and health.

Fear the LORD, rejoice in the LORD, delight in the Word. In due time, the LORD GOD shall provide. Provision comes from the LORD.

You shall be blessed in business.
Deuteronomy 28:3 Blessed shalt thou be in the city, and blessed shalt thou be in the field.

When you are living under the umbrella of blessings—everything in your life including business prosper. When you are in the market you shall outdo all your competition because the favor and the grace of GOD IS UPON YOU. In contrast, when you are in the curse, your land shall not yield an increase. People in the market will outdo you. The curse shall be upon your product till you break it in the name of the LORD. GOD does not despise sincere prayers from the heart. We call the heartfelt prayers. A curse is meant to be broken. Until it is broken, you will still be on a slave ship.

Good Health & prosperity.

Deuteronomy 28:4 Blessed shall be the fruit of thy body, and the fruit of thy ground, and the
fruit of thy cattle, the increase of thy kine, and the flocks of thy sheep.

Good health is as a result of obedience to the Word of GOD.

Psalm 119 :1-2 Blessed are the undefiled in the way, who walk in the law of the LORD.
Blessed are they that keep his testimonies, and that seek him with the whole heart.

Harkening unto the voice of the LORD is a healing unto our bodies.

Psalm 107:20 He sent his word, and healed them, and delivered them from their destructions.

When you are frequently battling strange diseases, one minute you're OK, the next you are ill, there are demons at play. There are times when you need medical attention and times when you need spiritual attention.

The LORD is your deliverer. Your refuge. When you are in CHRIST the plagues that befell Egyptians none shall be upon your body. The greatest healer of all time is JESUS CHRIST. He went to the cross so that you can be free in your body. Claim your healing in faith. Wealth and health shall be your portion and your inheritance in the name of the LORD. TRUST IN THE LORD FOR YOUR HEALING!

Psalm 112:3-4 Wealth and riches shall be in his house: and his righteousness endureth forever.
Unto the upright there ariseth light in the darkness: he is gracious, and full of compassion, and righteous.

You enemies shall be smitten.

Deuteronomy 28: 7 The LORD shall cause thine enemies that rise up against thee to be
smitten before thy face: they shall come out against thee one way, and flee before thee seven ways.

Like Joshua, no one in your days shall be able to stand you. The enemy defeats us because we have open doors of attack in our lives. He can only attack where there are weaknesses. If your opponents know your weaknesses, they will focus on the spot till you are defeated.

Although, when you walk uprightly, the face of the LORD shall confuse the camp of your enemies. Their trap will not work on you. Witchcraft will not work on you. This is the heritage of those in CHRIST JESUS in spirit and truth.

We may not be talking about a physical fight but a spiritual one. By your prophetic decrees and declaration, the kingdom of darkness shall suffer the fate. The hand of the LORD was upon Joshua, and He conquered 7 nations. You shall conquer for the LORD GOD is your stronghold.

The righteous are bold like lions. Even if he falls, the LORD shall lift him. You shall be lifted in the name of the LORD. DO NOT DIM YOUR LIGHT!

You shall be called Holy People.

9 The LORD shall establish thee an holy people unto himself, as he hath sworn unto thee, if thou shalt keep the commandments of the LORD thy God,
and walk in his ways.

You shall lend, not borrow.

12 The LORD shall open unto thee his good treasure, the heaven to give the
rain unto thy land in his season, and to bless all the work of thine hand:
and thou
shalt lend unto many nations, and thou shalt not borrow
You shall be the head not the tail.

13 And the LORD shall make thee the head, and not the tail; and thou
shalt
be above only, and thou shalt not be beneath; if that thou hearken unto the
commandments of the LORD thy God, which I command thee this day, to
observe and to do them: 14 And thou shalt not go aside from any of the
words
which I command thee this day, to the right hand, or to the left, to go after
other
gods to serve them.

Cursed life of not walking in the ways of GOD.

Poverty and all kinds of sicknesses.

Deuteronomy 28:15 But it shall come to pass, if thou wilt not hearken unto the voice of the

LORD thy God, to observe to do all his commandments and his statutes which I

command thee this day; that all these curses shall come upon thee, and overtake

thee: 16 Cursed shalt thou be in the city, and cursed shalt thou be in the field.

17 Cursed shall be thy basket and thy store.

18 Cursed shall be the fruit of thy body, and the fruit of thy land, the increase of thy kine, and the flocks of thy sheep.

19 Cursed shalt thou be when thou comest in, and cursed shalt thou be when

thou goest out.

Non-achievement life.

The LORD shall send upon thee cursing, vexation, and rebuke, in all that thou settest thine hand unto for to do, until thou be destroyed, and until thou

perish quickly; because of the wickedness of thy doings, whereby thou hast forsaken me.

Closed heaven.

Deuteronomy 28:23 And thy heaven that is over thy head shall be brass, and the earth that is
under thee shall be iron.

Your enemies shall rule you.

Deuteronomy 28:25 The LORD shall cause thee to be smitten before thine enemies: thou shalt
go out one way against them, and flee seven ways before them: and shalt be removed into all the kingdoms of the earth.

Oppression & slavery.

Deuteronomy 28:29 And thou shalt grope at noonday, as the blind gropeth in darkness, and
thou shalt not prosper in thy ways: and thou shalt be only oppressed and spoiled
evermore, and no man shall save thee.

GOD is the ultimate light of every man and woman. We choose darkness by cutting our ties with Him through living and going by our own rule. When we reject the HOLY SPIRIT, we make it clear that we love darkness more than light.

We know the history of men and women who rejected the Law of GOD. Slavery was their portion. Even to this day, the spirit of slavery is still as powerful as it was yesterday. Some people are slaves of their own selves, unable to accept who they are, some are slaves spiritually, bound by the powers of darkness, slaves for the culture and traditions of this world. Above all, many are mentally enslaved by the evil system of this world ruled by the god of this world.

You can be a slave to power, money, fame, etc. anything that overrules you, controls you, owns you. You are under the bondage of it. As I look at my country, South Africa, millions are under the bondage of poverty, unemployment, and alcohol. This is not a closed call, just a few. Apart from looking at it from a narrow view, in a global landscape, the vicious demonic issue is mind control. It does not matter which race, language, color, or culture you represent, the anti-Christ spirit is dominating the world—perpetrating through mind control.

Be saved in the LORD. Folks, let us go back to the CREATOR.

Non-marriage life, no happiness, non-family life.
Deuteronomy 28: 30 Thou shalt betroth a wife, and another man shall lie with her: thou shalt
build an house, and thou shalt not dwell therein: thou shalt plant a vineyard, and
shalt not gather the grapes thereof.

Many struggle in this line. You find it difficult to keep a relationship, or if you are married, there is no peace and happiness. It is a back-and-forth type relationship, with unnecessary arguments and fights from time to time, know that you are dealing with spirits. Deliverance is needed, and above all, total surrender to the will of GOD.

Usually, generational curse affects marriage more than other areas. Adultery is the cause of this issue. If you study the life of David, after he committed murder and adultery, his house after his has never had peace. Struggled with adultery and the sword was never spared in his house. The judgment of GOD comes when we disobey the principles He has placed.

Disobedience to the voice of GOD has consequences. It is the principle of "Reaping what you sow".

Lack and favor shall not be with you.
Deuteronomy 28:38 Thou shalt carry much seed out into the field, and shalt gather but little
in; for the locust shall consume it.

When you do not have luck and the favor of GOD in your life, everything you touch does not profit and multiply. Remember, we are called to walk in dominion, to subdue, to be fruitful, and to multiply in all things, not just in making babies.

Weapons of Spiritual warfare.

Ephesians 6:12 For we wrestle not against flesh and blood, but against principalities, against powers, against the rulers of the darkness of this world, against spiritual wickedness in high places.

There are unseen realms that are more real and active similar to this world. And the fight does not require our physical strength but spiritual power. That spiritual power is available to you in Christ. Christ is the head of the church, a mighty man of war, who spoiled principalities and powers of evil and brought them to shame. It is your duty as the child of the Most High to enforce Christ's victory in your life. From this scripture above, we can tell that the kingdom of Satan is organized. Some principalities are powerful demons assigned over countries, powers over regions or provinces, and rulers of the darkness of this world are those fallen spirits that rule over sea, earth, and the underworld.

You have to understand that when the devil fell, he took a third of the angels with him. That will make about millions of fallen angels and billions of demons that are against you. But take heart, we have more on our side. The powerful archangel Michael defeated Lucifer, now called the deceiver.

Revelation 12:7 And there was war in heaven: Michael and his angels fought against the dragon; and the dragon fought and his angels, 8 And prevailed not; neither was their place found any more in heaven. 9 And the great dragon was cast out, that old serpent, called the Devil, and Satan, which deceiveth the whole world: he was cast out into the earth, and his angels were cast out with him.

The first war started in heaven. Iniquity was found in Lucifer and he was no longer able to be in the presence of God—his form was not the same. Pride was found in him. He wanted to do his own thing and have his kingdom like the Most High. Ezekiel 28 and Isaiah 14 have more to say about the cause of his fall. It was the archangel Michael, the prince over the nation of Israel, who defeated the Devil and his angels.

This took place in the third heaven—this is the dwelling place of the MOST HIGH GOD. Through divine spiritual experiences I had, I without a doubt, attest that there a three heavens. The first heaven is the literal space we see with our naked eyes, while the second heaven is the space between the first and third heaven. The third heaven is the final destination of the saints of God. This is the dwelling place of the MOST HIGH GOD, Christ, the hope of our glory, saints, and angels.

This is your place of authority when you engage in spiritual warfare with the forces of darkness. Know that you're seated with CHRIST in heavenly places. All you have to do is believe and exercise your authority in CHRIST. There are so many evil things that get you off the track with your maker, but never give it in. Resist the enemy and he shall free from you.

Hebrews 11:6 But without faith it is impossible to please him: for he that cometh to God must believe that he is, and that he is a rewarder of them that diligently seek him.

Faith is your heavenly key to dismantling the power of darkness in your life. This is the power that comes from the gospel of salvation. Faith in God will lead you to victory in all things. Jesus Christ values faith. Jesus responds according to your faith. Exercise your faith and see the salvation of the Lord.

James 4:7 Submit yourselves therefore to God. Resist the devil, and he will flee from you.

Total submission to the Lord is the only way you are going to be covered and shielded from all demonic forces. You don't have to be half-Christian and half-world at the same time. Trust in the Lord only. Submit your spirit, soul, and body under the Lordship of our good shepherd Christ.

Ephesians 2:6 And hath raised us up together, and made us sit together in heavenly places in Christ Jesus:

One's power is determined by who is his headship. Our headship is Christ. This is the power that is above any other power in this world and in the world to come. I plead with you to be all fired up for Christ. And for the salvation that only comes through the gospel of Christ. This world does not sleep. Evil is at high more than ever. Temptation here and there, but never take your eyes off Christ. Men and women fall when they take their eyes off Christ. This is what Apostle Peter experienced when walking on water. He took the step of faith to do something he had never done or could never think of doing, he was doing good until fear started gripping him. It started when he took his eyes away from Christ.

Moses was commanded to make a bronze snake. And to place it upon a pole. Whoever looked on the snake who was bitten by the snake was healed. Faith starts off when you look above where the eternal source of all things resides.

Psalm 121:1-2 I will lift up mine eyes unto the hills, from whence cometh my help. 2 My help cometh from the LORD, which made heaven and earth.

Spiritual warfare is a spiritual battle between good and evil. These are forces of evil against the forces of good. And our ultimate enemy is the Devil himself. In any way the Devil will never be equal to God, our God is Almighty. Lately, the enemy has been popularized and glorified as if he is all mighty. That is not the case with the devil. He is not omnipotent and omniscient like God is. He cannot be anywhere and everywhere at the same time. He is just an organizational personality who has subordinates under his evil rulership.

Christ came so that we might have life and live a victorious life in all aspects of our lives. The enemy, Satan, his mission is to kill, steal, and destroy humankind. He has an intact kingdom assisted by fallen angels and demons to destroy your life. But the good news is that he is already defeated.

Psalm 108:13 Through God we shall do valiantly: for he it is that shall tread down our enemies.

Ephesians 4: 8 Wherefore he saith, When he ascended up on high, he led captivity captive, and gave gifts unto men.

The death and resurrection of Christ liberated us from the spiritual prisons of the hands of the rulers of darkness. Freedom comes from the truth. The way, the truth, and life is none but Christ. Who came in the name of the Lord.

Psalm 118:22 The stone which the builders refused is become the head stone of the corner. 23 This is the LORD's doing; it is marvellous in our eyes. 24 This is the day which the LORD hath made; we will rejoice and be glad in it.

Psalm 118:26 Blessed be he that cometh in the name of the LORD: we have blessed you out of the house of the LORD.

Power of worship.

This is my favorite chapter so far. I love worship so much. We are called in this kingdom to worship the MOST HIGH. Abraham was well-received and loved because he was a worshipper. GOD is looking for true worshippers. Those who worship Him in the spirit of truth and sincere heart.

I strongly believe that you cannot move into a greater dimension of the glory of GOD if you are not a worshipper. JESUS CHRIST worshipped the Father. JESUS CHRIST praised the Father of all things. And taught us the way to the heart of the Father.

Psalm 100:4-5 Enter into his gates with thanksgiving, and into his courts
with praise: be
thankful unto him, and bless his name.
5 For the LORD is good; his mercy is everlasting; and his truth endureth
to
all generations.

First and foremost, when you approach the LIVING KING, it is a must to offer thanksgiving for He is a great KING. And He has done so much in your life. Even if you feel like you have nothing to be thankful for, be thankful that you are still breathing. Be thankful that you can still smile. Be thankful for the gifts, talents, and skills that the LORD GOD has blessed you with. We are all blessed with all spiritual blessings in the heavenly places. Likewise, with earthy gifts and talents.

The angels in the heavens do not get tired of giving thanks and honor unto the LORD. Some things just need you to be grateful. This is the first step of greater things in life—gratitude. Secondly, we enter His court with praise.

I can write the whole book just with the phrase "Praise". Praise is a weapon of spiritual warfare. We praise Him so that we can be saved. He is enthroned even higher when we lift up our voices in praise. He inhabits the praises of his people (Psalm 22:3). The glory will never be the house that praises. The glory would never leave the house that worships in spirit and truth.

Brethren, I urge you to be like King David who moves the heart of GOD through his sincere praise and worship. At some point, He even forgot that he was the king of Israel, somewhere even making a mockery of Him for dancing before the LORD.

The LORD is to be praised and honored from the sun rising to the sun setting. Why? Because HE IS A GREAT KING!

GOD created man in his own image, in the image of GOD he created him; male and female he created them. We worship God by mirroring Him. Mirroring Him is by constantly opening our ears to hear what the HOLY SPIRIT says. You will be surprised that the greatest miracles that JESUS performed, He gave thanks unto the LORD beforehand with the assurance of a positive outcome. The perfect example is the miracle of Lazarus "He looked unto the heavens and gave thanks, and he called out the dead man to life". It can only be the power of worship—seeing things from GOD's perspective—moving when GOD is moving.

Hold on unto the small still voice of the LORD. HOLY SPIRIT is your friend in need. He will help us to be in tune with the mind and the will of GOD. When your mind is set on things above where GOD dwells and the power of worship, your mind will be transformed into light. The light of GOD is a new perspective, understanding, drop of knowledge, and wisdom.

It is vital to surrender your mind and will to GOD especially when you are dealing with generation curses. The power is to turn away from worshipping things other than GOD. Media, music, entertainment, and social media are today's idols. Putting them above the wisdom of GOD is foolishness.

Let us go into His presence with a sincere heart and contrite spirit, the wheel of every car that the enemy has been driving shall overturn. There is power in worship, but the worship is in the spirit of truth.

John 4:23-24 But the hour cometh, and now is, when the true worshippers shall
worship the Father in spirit and in truth: for the Father seeketh such to worship
him.
24 God is a Spirit: and they that worship him must worship him in spirit and
in truth.

JESUS made it clear to the Samaritan women that it does not matter where you worship but when the hour cometh for worship, you must worship in spirit and truth. Meaning, your sincere worship must come from within. Within your heart is where the HOLY SPIRIT is moving and at work. Worship is a prayer. It must be heartfelt. And it must certainly reflect the Word of GOD. When you pray, you must pray the Word of GOD back to Him. In saying, that is, to pray the will of GOD. If you are outside the will of GOD, surely it will be a vain prayer.

Aron, the brother of Moses, was told to keep the light on in the temple of GOD. This is a symbol of our prayer life. We should never give up the lifestyle of prayer. Worship is a sweet aroma in the nostrils of GOD. When He smelled the sacrifices of Noah after the flood, He vowed to never destroy the earth by floods again—a rainbow was an emblem of his testament.

Genesis 8:20-22 And Noah builded an altar unto the LORD; and took of every clean
beast, and of every clean fowl, and offered burnt offerings on the altar.
21 And the LORD smelled a sweet savour; and the LORD said in his heart, I
will not again curse the ground any more for man's sake; for the imagination of
man's heart is evil from his youth; neither will I again smite any more every thing living, as I have done.

22 While the earth remaineth, seedtime and harvest, and cold and heat, and

summer and winter, and day and night shall not cease.

A sweet savor is the aura of worship. A worshipper will always have a place in the heart of the MOST HIGH. And a worshipper will have many enemies—trying to bring him down like David. But through worship and praise, He shall be saved. The enemy does want the praise and worship adoration to go to GOD.

Psalm 18:3 I will call upon the LORD, who is worthy to be praised: so shall I be

saved from mine enemies.

Besides worship being an act of service to GOD, worship are song of deliverance. If you want to be delivered from marine evil strongholds, demonic addictions, witchcraft, and other satanic ties—Worship! When they were going to fight in Judah during the reign of Jehoshaphat, they went to the battle with anointed musical instruments singing "His mercy endures forever".

Psalm 118:1-4 O give thanks unto the LORD; for he is good: because his mercy endureth

for ever.

2 Let Israel now say, that his mercy endureth for ever.

3 Let the house of Aaron now say, that his mercy endureth for ever.

4 Let them now that fear the LORD say, that his mercy endureth for ever.

There was a shift in the realm of spirit when they praised the MOST HIGH. It was no longer Judah fighting but the angel of GOD amidst the battle helping Israel.

Psalm 22:3 But thou art holy, O thou that inhabitest the praises of Israel.

It is safe to say that during spiritual warfare battle—praise and worship are the greatest weapons given to mankind. No demon can block the power force energy of a worshipper. Worship is a demon destroyer. Demons cannot stand the fire. Fire is around you when you worship. Even the atmosphere of your territory changes when you worship, sing, and praise the great KING!

The impossible write possible with GOD.

Worship is war.

When we worship God, we are engaged in spiritual warfare against the demonic realm. We read of Jesus Christ, "the devil took him to a very high mountain and showed him all the kingdoms of the world and their glory. And he said to him, 'All these I will give you, if you will fall down and worship me.' Then Jesus said to him, "Be gone, Satan! For it is written, 'You shall worship the Lord your God and him only shall you serve.'

Both the Father and Satan offered Jesus the same opportunity - to sit at their right-hand ruling and reigning over a kingdom in power. The difference was that Satan offered the pleasure path, and the Father offered the pain path. Jesus' choice was an act of war, as He would either choose to worship Satan and war against the Father or choose to worship the Father and war against Satan.

We make the same choice every day. Jesus saw all of the collective sinful temptations that everyone was facing on planet Earth. Today, technology and the internet allow us to do the same. We can see global sex, fame, power, money, possessions, and pleasures in an instant and this is all a demonic war for the soul of the world as Satan wants to be worshipped through idolatry.

God creates, and Satan counterfeits. The counterfeit of worship is idolatry. When Paul and Silas were put in prison, at midnight they chose to war in spirit—worshipping and praising GOD. The mighty Angel of GOD descended with power on them, and the foundation of the prisons was shaken, and the chain fell. What is interesting is that even the other prisoner's chain of those who were not part of the worship fell, and were delivered. This is the power of GOD!

"May the praise of God be in their mouths and a double-edged sword in their hands."

(Psalm 149:6)

Worship gives us the ability to enter into a heavenly realm where we gain strength, confidence, and vision to overcome the challenges we face in the earthly realm. The praise of God in our mouths is like a double-edged sword through which we conquer our enemies.

Word of GOD.

The Word is the sword of the spirit. The Word is powerful. Many won't believe that even in the kingdom of darkness they highly regard the Bible as the Word of the LIVING GOD. Satan knows the Word more than us. He studies the Word to deceive and manipulate. Even demons know the words more than us. It is a fact.

The Devil cannot operate of the scope of the bible, whatsoever that is written of him, he walks in the same line. He knows that his end is not yet, thus, he has to take as many souls down with Him. And he does this with many human agents, fallen angels, and demons he has to destroy Christians.

Without the Word and the Spirit of CHRIST, we are no match for the kingdom of darkness. Don't be deceived, the kingdom of darkness has power. They harness the power of the darkness—manipulating even the sun, moon, and constellations to work against humanity. It is the government of disruption and destruction upon humankind.

Throughout my walk with GOD, I have noticed two things that weaken our walk with GOD; and that is ignorance and disobedience of the Word of GOD. A witch or wizard can quote scriptures randomly like nobody's business, come a Christian believer, or she/he will only tell you about John 3:16 and a few basic foundations.

This year 2024, we should move away from church culture to GOD faith. Move away from the world culture to GOD CULTURE, which is the WORD. Scripture meditation should be the norm. Word memorization should be the norm. holiness and righteousness to be upholded even in the day and age of grace. In the age of grace, we move up higher like John was called to climb up high. To go in higher realms and dimensions—taking back what the enemy has stolen from our fathers.

We should be like Gideon's generation to uproot and destroy the altars of demonic shrines. Christianity should be seen through your character of righteousness and act of selflessness. An act of humility can open doors you never thought would. Life is a war. We are in constant battle with the forces with cannot see with our naked eye.

Thanks to the MOST HIGH, who has blessed us with all spiritual wisdom, knowledge, and understanding. If it wasn't for the grace of the LORD, I wouldn't be writing this book to you. This book is a testament to the grace and mercy of GOD upon my life. My testimony is your testimony. We overcome Satan by the blood of the lamb and by our testimony. Testimony testifies to what the LORD has done.

It testifies that His mercy endures forever. The Word of GOD testifies about JESUS CHRIST. In faith when you release the Word out of your mouth, it is empowered by the mighty SPIRIT OF GOD. It is the spirit that does all things. The gifting comes from the spirit. the spirit preceded from the Father. To strengthen the saints and believers in their God-given assignment.

Everything that you need in this world is in the Word. We must approach the word of GOD the way Daniel did. He studied the word with understanding. He prayed for understanding to decode the sacred meaning of the scriptures. And he prayed according to the scripture. It is written that after he understood the prophecy in the book of the prophet Jeremiah, he set his face unto the LORD. What if he did not understand the prophecy? He would have been still in the same position.

Understanding comes from the HOLY SPIRIT. if you take the HOLY SPIRIT out of the context of the word, you will get nothing but information. But when the veil is unveiled, it is a revelation!

Even in the anatomy of deliverance, the Word of GOD is the pillar.

Hebrews 4:12 For the word of God is quick, and powerful, and sharper than any twoedged sword, piercing even to the dividing asunder of soul and spirit, and of the joints and marrow, and is a discerner of the thoughts and intents of the heart.

2 Corinthians 10: 3 For though we walk in the flesh, we do not war after the flesh: 4 (For the weapons of our warfare are not carnal, but mighty

Psalm 1:2 But his delight is in the law of the LORD; and in his law doth he meditate day and night.

Joshua 1:8 This book of the law shall not depart out of thy mouth; but thou shalt meditate therein day and night, that thou mayest observe to do according to all that is written therein: for then thou shalt make thy way prosperous, and then thou shalt have good success.

When you pray the word, you automatically pray the will of God. When the Lord of host says come let us reason together in the book of Isaiah, He means through His word. It means our prayers have to be backed up by His word. It is His word that justifies us. You can never go wrong praying what you know to be the will of the Father. Christ came to do the will of His Father, and so are we.

Day to day we should live by the truth of GOD. There are so many manipulations, lies, and deceptions in this world. Your mind is the most important aspect of your body. Your reasoning capability, critical decision, and your worldview can be shaped by your mind. Enlarge your mind with the truth of GOD, which is His Word. You shall never fall. The fall of every man happens when he drifts away from the Word. The Word is food for your soul, spirit, and body.

Fellowship with other Believers.

13 And the decree went forth that the wise men should be slain; and they sought Daniel and his fellows to be slain.
14 Then Daniel answered with counsel and wisdom to Arioch the captain of the king's guard, which was gone forth to slay the wise men of Babylon:
15 He answered and said to Arioch the king's captain, Why is the decree so hasty from the king? Then Arioch made the thing known to Daniel.
16 Then Daniel went in, and desired of the king that he would give him time, and that he would shew the king the interpretation.
17 Then Daniel went to his house, and made the thing known to Hananiah, Mishael, and Azariah, his companions:
18 That they would desire mercies of the God of heaven concerning this secret; that Daniel and his fellows should not perish with the rest of the wise men of Babylon.
19 Then was the secret revealed unto Daniel in a night vision. Then Daniel blessed the God of heaven (Daniel 2:13-19).

We often assume that Daniel on his own prayed and the secret was revealed unto him. It was more of a collective prayer. GOD was merciful to redeem the lives of every prophet, diviner, soothsayer, necromancy, and astrologist through the prayers of Daniel, Shadrack, Meshach, and Abednego.

The hand of mercy was upon Babylon because GOD was coming to them through Daniel and his friends. Their unshakable faith was a testimony throughout the land of Babylon that the GOD of the heavens rules all. Yet the land was filled with strange gods and goddesses worshipped everywhere like India. In India, the shrines of gods and goddesses are on the road, people can pray to them anywhere, at home, on the road, etc. Thus, was Babylon.

It was culture. But our GOD is above culture and traditions. Thus, Daniel rose in power over the witches and wizards of the land. He was ten times better than all the wise of the Babylon kingdom because the spirit of wisdom, understanding, and knowledge was upon Him. Even the spirit of excellency.

I am talking about Daniel because he is the perfect example of fellowship. He had Shadrack, Meshach, and Abednego—the men of great faith in his life to strengthen each other in matters of faith. We know that the journey of faith is difficult. It is good to have good friends you can pray with, study with, and enjoy the company with. That even in difficult times, they will strengthen that soul to never weaken.

We can also talk about the friendship between David and Jonathan. It was a godly friendship. Fellowshipping with other believers is important especially when you are in a season of spiritual attack from the enemy. When death knocks on it door in your family, they will be there to support and comfort your soul. When marriage is hitting rock bottom, good friends will be there.

It is truly difficult to find such people of the caliber of Shadrack, Meshach, and Abednego, who will stand the test of time with their faith. These three men made the GOD of Israel famous throughout the land of Babylon if I may say, that the nation started calling GOD after their name "GOD of Shadrack, Meshach, and Abednego.

In the old days, people used to call him "The GOD of Shadrack, Meshach, and Abednego, especially when going through the fire—trials, and tribulations.

1 But now thus saith the LORD that created thee, O Jacob, and he that formed thee, O Israel, Fear not: for I have redeemed thee, I have called thee by
thy name; thou art mine.
2 When thou passest through the waters, I will be with thee; and through the

rivers, they shall not overflow thee: when thou walkest through the fire,
thou
shalt not be burned; neither shall the flame kindle upon thee.

This is what happened to Shadrack, Meshach, and Abednego, the flame did not kindle them nor was any smell of fire upon their garments. They totally surrendered to the will of GOD for not bowing to other gods.

Psalm 95:3 For the LORD is a great God, and a great King above all gods.

The LORD GOD is able to save you from destruction. You just have to keep the faith and believe the unbelievable. Men and women who believed were counted as righteous even though they lived a sinful life. Faith is power. Faith is action. Faith is your ticket to the greatest. It goes along with obedience. Obedient faith will get you results. CHRIST honors faith. He was moved when individuals displayed faith.

Faith is the issue of the heart. Believing the unknown, however, in line with the will of GOD. If it says yes in the Word of GOD, then the answer is amen. It cometh by hearing the Word of GOD. Rich in the Word, rich in faith. Never listen to any other voice that does not lead to the promised land.

There are so many voices. But the LORD of peace will manifest himself unto you. Exercise and stir up the spirit of discerning. Darkness has covered the world. But the mighty spirit of CHRIST in you is the light of the Word. Be fearless. Be encouraged and inspired by the LORD. The LORD is great and above all other strange gods.

You shall live and not die, and see the promises of GOD in your lifetime. This is what the spirit of the LORD says. Guard your heart and your mind. Scripture meditation will transform your mind and thoughts so as to be in line with GOD. The impossible writes possible with GOD.

Life is spiritual. Life is a war. But we are already overcomers in the name of JESUS. The name of JESUS is great for this age and age to come. He is the WORD. In heaven, or in spirit, He is the WORD of power and glory. No man dead or alive is greater than JESUS CHRIST THE SON

OF THE LIVING GOD. Be comforted. Be healed. Be restored. All in the name of the LORD GOD MOST HIGH IN CHRIST.

HALLELUAH!

GLORY TO YAH.

Repentance is king!

Psalm 51:1-7 Have mercy upon me, O God, according to thy loving kindness: according unto the multitude of thy tender mercies blot out my transgressions. 2 Wash me throughly from mine iniquity, and cleanse me from my sin. 3 For I acknowledge my transgressions: and my sin is ever before me. 4 Against thee, thee only, have I sinned, and done this evil in thy sight: that thou mightest be justified when thou speakest, and be clear when thou judgest. 5 Behold, I was shapen in iniquity; and in sin did my mother conceive me. 6 Behold, thou desirest truth in the inward parts: and in the hidden part thou shalt make me to know wisdom. 7 Purge me with hyssop, and I shall be clean: wash me, and I shall be whiter than snow.

Repentance is the soldier 's weapon of defence and attack. When you are riding on a clean slate with Christ, you can come boldly to the throne of grace with your petition and have confidence that it shall be added unto you. Sin opens doors to demonic attacks. It grants the accuser of our brethren a legal right to wreck our lives to the ground. The Devil does not have love for anyone. Whether be it to his government or his human agents. Don't be fooled when he calls you his son. He will at all-time wage warfare with mankind who resembles the face of the spirit of the LIVING GOD.

I come from a church that was serving Lucifer. I was fooled by the majority of following the so-called man of God. Many of us believers tend to go by our senses rather than spirit. There is a difference between natural senses and spiritual senses. There is also a difference between confidence and faith. The greatest weapon of this end age is the spirit of discernment. This will save many of us from wondering if it is the voice of God or the devil. These are the two kingdoms in rivalry, the kingdom of God and the kingdom of the Devil.

The two great graces essential to a believer in this life are faith and repentance. These are the two which grant us the ticket to eternal life with God. Faith and repentance preserve the spiritual life just as heat and radical moisture preserve the natural. The grace which I am going to discuss is repentance.

Total deliverance is repentance from the sins of our forefathers and our own. When we are under sin the enemy can do what he pleases. The enemy of your heart—the devil will bombard you with a host of demonic attacks whenever there is access to your soul through sin.

Repentance is a grace required under the gospel. Some think it legal; but the first sermon that Christ preached, indeed, the first word of his sermon, was "Repent" (Mat 4.17). And his farewell that he left when he was going to ascend was that "repentance should be preached in his name" (Luk 24.47). The apostles went on to preach the same message "(Mar 6.12).

Repentance is about gospel grace. The covenant of works allowed no repentance; there it was: sin and die. Repentance came in by the gospel. Christ has purchased us through his blood so that repenting sinners can be saved. The law required personal, perfect, and perpetual obedience. It cursed all who could not come up to this: "Cursed is everyone that does not continue to do all things which are written in the book of the law" (Gal 3.10). It does not say, "He that does not obey all things, let him repent;" instead, it says "Let him be cursed." Thus repentance is a doctrine that has been brought to light only by the gospel.

I have always viewed repentance as warfare against the kingdom of the darkness. The enemy leaves you when you come clean with God. Though he will try you to see if you won't go back to your old ways. Repenting is coming back to your Father's house once again. It is a way of life. The beautiful journey of life is a road of no perfection on our part but from God. God is the cup of our salvation—our robe of righteousness.

You will never lose a fight if you can be a man of repentance. Look at David, through his shortfalls and shortcomings, God was able to restore, revive, and forgive him. The life of David is a picture of God's mercy and grace. We do not deserve grace but we deserve mercy. Grace is a virtue from God. Our God is a gracious Lord. Compassionate. Kind.

Biblically we understand that because of the rebellion of the fall of man, we need redemption. Without the renewing of the Holy Spirit, spiritually speaking, our hearts were corruptible so God had to call us to repent! It can only be the work of God. Humility is the first step to repentance.

"Therefore say unto the house of Israel, Thus saith the Lord God; Repent, and turn yourselves from your idols; and turn away your faces from all your abominations." Ezekiel 14:6

"And saying, Repent ye: for the kingdom of heaven is at hand." Matthew 3:2

"I tell you, Nay: but, except ye repent, ye shall all likewise perish." Luke 13:3

"The Lord is not slack concerning his promise, as some men count slackness; but is longsuffering to us-ward, not willing that any should perish, but that all should come to repentance." 2 Peter 3:9 (KJV)

Curse breaking prayers.

Heavenly Father, I confess the following sins and iniquities for myself and my family line.

Please forgive me and my family line. I bind all demonic forces operating around me and my family line.

I repent and renounce the spirits of fear and anxiety, as well as their controlling factors in my life and the lives of my ancestors.

I choose faith over fear. I repent and renounce word curses spoken from my mouth, including condemnations, judgments, curses, and ungodly covenants. I break off all such curses spoken by my ancestors from my family line.

I repent and renounce guilt, shame, and condemnation.

I repent and renounce all forms of pride.

I repent and renounce my anger and bitterness. I choose to bless those toward whom I have harbored anger and bitterness.

I repent and renounce my hatred of others, including hatred against men or women or people of other skin colors. I break off these curses of hatred from myself and my family line.

I repent and renounce broken families through divorce and promiscuity. I break this curse off myself and my family.

I repent and renounce the spirit of poverty and the influence it has over my finances and the finances of my family line. I choose from this day forward to be obedient with God's provision and finances.

I repent and renounce ungodly associations, vows, covenants, and secret handshakes.

I repent and renounce all involvement in the occult, witchcraft, and the New Age by me and my family. I forgive my family of their sins and their involvement in these ungodly beliefs.

I repent and renounce having sought and used supernatural powers, levitation, out-of-body experiences, psychics, spells, rituals, and ungodly blood covenants. I break off all curses from myself and my family.

I repent and renounce the religious spirit and the spirit of rebellion.

I repent and renounce all of my involvement and my family's involvement in Freemasonry and the Daughter of the Eastern Star. I break all curses and renounce all vows, from the 1st to the 33rd Degree of Freemasonry. I renounce all oaths of Eastern Star secrecy and silence. I forgive my family of their sins, known and unknown, and of their involvement in this.

I repent and renounce all vows, handshakes, blood oaths, and rituals of the Mormon Church. I renounce satan and his messenger spirit Morani and his false revelation. I renounce the ceremonies of the Mormon temple. I forgive my family of their sins and unknown sins and involvement in this.

I repent and renounce my involvement and my family's involvement with the Jehovah's Witnesses. I repent for all false and religious doctrines. I ask forgiveness for the rejection of the Holy Spirit. I forgive my family of their sins and unknown sins and involvement in this.

I repent and renounce all feelings of rejection from my mother, father, husband or wife, and family members. I break off the spirit of rejection in my life. I repent for feeling orphaned and unwanted. I repent for the destruction it has caused my family and me. I confess these sins and break them from my family line. Please forgive me of these sins.

I repent for feelings of hating myself. I know I was beautifully and wonderfully created. Any and all lies about my being inadequate in any way are from Satan. Jesus, please forgive me for having these feelings and for wanting to hurt myself. I renounce these thoughts and break them off my family line and me.

I repent and renounce sexual sin by me and my family. Please forgive me of my sins and my family's iniquities of sexual promiscuity, ritual sex, pornography, masturbation, rape, obsessive or unnatural desires of lust, homosexuality, sexual abuse, incest, and sex with animals. I break off the assignment of the spirit of perversion and the religious spirit off me and my family line.

I break off all soul ties passed to my family and me by sex partners, adultery, and premarital sex that have entered into my family line.

I repent and renounce all word curses that I have spoken myself and from my ancestors. I replace these word curses with blessings. Please forgive me.

I repent and renounce having an abortion or being the responsible male for getting a woman pregnant and paying for the abortion. I repent of my lack of consideration of human life. I confess these sins and I ask forgiveness.

I repent and renounce word curses pronounced by me or my ancestors. I cancel these curses and replace them with blessings. Father, please forgive me and my family line.

I repent and renounce all verbal and physical abuse against myself and my family. I renounce the destruction that it has caused my family and myself. I choose to no longer be a victim and I now identify the lies of Satan. Please forgive me for being a victim. I choose to live free under the miraculous work of Jesus Christ.

I repent and renounce having verbally and physically abused and harmed others. I confess my sins in these areas and I ask for forgiveness. Father, please forgive my family and me for any and all involvement in both physical and verbal abuse.

I repent and renounce any and all untimely deaths in my family. Sickness and death are from Satan. I repent for blaming You, God. Please forgive me. I break off all curses and assignments of death over my family.

I repent and renounce the spirit of poverty over my family and me.

I break off the assignment of poverty over my finances, my family's finances, and my manner of thinking. Please forgive me.

I repent and renounce my feelings of blame toward myself, other people, and You, God. I confess my sin of blaming others and You. Please forgive me, Lord for blaming myself, others, and You, God.

Heavenly Father, I choose to live free today. I release myself and my family from these curses, and any and all generational curses. I choose to have Your blessings released on me and my family today, and from this day forward, in Jesus' name!

BLESSING PRAYERS.

Let the rivers of blessings flow unto me from the north.
Let the rivers of blessings flows unto me from the east.
Let the rivers of blessings flows unto me from the west.
Let the rivers of blessings flows unto me from the south.
I am the center of blessings.
I am abundantly blessed beyond measures in the name of the LORD.
As Abraham was blessed, so shall I be blessed through CHRIST.
AS Solomon was blessed, so shall I be blessed in CHRIST.
As David was blessed, so shall I be blessed in the name of the LORD.
Light be in my life.
Light be in my family.
Light be in my career.
Light be in my ministry.
Light be in my marriage.
Light be in my children.
The light arises in the darkness for me.
Light in the darkness is my LORD, My Savior.
Let my prayers unto you be as sweet as aroma.
Let me live under the banner of your glory.
Spirit of GOD moves upon the face of my life.
Spirit of GOD moves upon the face of my ministry.
Spirit of GOD moves upon the face of my family.
Spirit of GOD moves upon the face of my finances.
Spirit of GOD moves upon the face of my marriage.
Spirit of GOD moves upon my body.
Spirit of GOD within me is the hope of my salvation.
Earth, bring forth my blessings in the name of the LORD.
Earth, bring forth my wealth in the name of the LORD.
Earth, bring forth my breakthrough in finances in the name of the
CREATOR.

Earth, bring forth healing leaves for my body in the name of JESUS CHRIST.

Earth, bring forth pleasing food unto me in the name of the LORD GOD.

I Speak the spirit of restoration upon everything the earth has swallowed unto my life in the name of JESUS CHRIST.

I speak the spirit of restoration upon every blessed swallowed by the earth in the mighty name of the LORD GOD OF GLORY.

Spirit of restoration and resurrection speaks for my spoiled blessing in the mighty name of JESUS.

Every evil tree planted to bring my family in bondage of non-achievement and poverty, be destroyed by the fire of GOD of Elijah right now.

GOD of fire. Destroy every evil tree planted that is speaking negatively upon my life.

Every tree that the LORD has not planted in my life, be uprooted in the name of the LORD OF HOST.

Fire of my prayer altar, destroy every power of darkness hovering my territory in the name of JESUS.

Every hidden spiritual marriage be destroyed by the power of the blood of JESUS.

My hands and my fingers are covered by the blood of JESUS.

My right ear is sprinkled with the blood of the lamb.

My right hand is sprinkled with the blood of the lamb.

My right toe is sprinkled with the blood of the lamb.

My soul, spirit, and body are covered with the power of the precious blood of the lamb.

By faith, I drink the power of the blood of JESUS CHRIST.

By faith I destroy every demon in my stomach, I drink the power of the blood of JESUS CHRIST.

I eat the flesh of JESUS CHRIST by faith.

I drink the blood of JESUS CHRIST by faith.

No weapon formed against me shall prosper in the mighty name of the LORD.
I overthrow every demonic altar that is speaking evil over my life in the name of JESUS CHRIST.
I silence the voice of every witch and wizard in the mighty name of JESUS CHRIST.
I cause confusion upon the camp of my enemies in the mighty name of JESUS CHRIST.
I rebuke you spirit of poverty in the mighty name of JESUS CHRIST.
I rebuke you spirit of mental slavery in the mighty name of JESUS CHRIST.
I rebuke you spirit of empty pockets in the mighty name of JESUS CHRIST.
I rebuke you spirit of witchcraft in the mighty name of JESUS CHRIST.
I rebuke you spirit laziness in the mighty name of JESUS CHRIST.
I rebuke you spirit of hopelessness in the mighty name of JESUS CHRIST.
The sun and the moon shall rule over the day of my life in peace in the name of JESUS CHRIST.
The sun and the moon shall not smite me in the name of JESUS CHRIST.
The sun and the moon shall not bring curse unto my life in the mighty name of JESUS CHRIST.
The heavenly hosts were created for my blessing.
I shake off curses placed over the sun and the moon the mighty name of JESUS CHRIST.
JESUS CHRIST rules over the cosmos for my blessings.
JESUS CHRIST rules over the planets and constellations for my blessings.
JESUS CHRIST rules over the sun and the moon to not smite me.
The sun and the moon shall be blessings unto my life.

The arrays of the sun shall heal me in the mighty name of JESUS CHRIST.

I speak open heaven over my life.
I speak mighty angels over my life.
I speak the angels of blessing over my life.
I speak angels of peace over my life.
I speak the angels of wealth over my life.
The angels of the LORD minister unto me.
The angels of the LORD comfort me.
The Angels of the LORD protect me.
The angels of the LORD guide me.
The angels of the LORD bless me.
I have dominion over the waters in the mighty name of JESUS CHRIST.
I have dominion over the land in the mighty name of JESUS CHRIST.
I have dominion over the fowls of the air in the mighty name of JESUS CHRIST.
I have dominion over principalities in the name of JESUS CHRIST.
I am seated in the heavenly places with CHRIST far above.
I have dominion over Satan and his demons in the mighty name of JESUS CHRIST.
By the blood of the lamb, I am more than a conqueror.
I am free in the mighty name of JESUS CHRIST!
Amen!!!!

Conclusion

I am blessed and honored for reading up this far. Be blessed. I hope this information provided in this book lead you into deeper experience with the Divine GOD. Follow me for more material like this. Stay blessed!

Notes.

Gene B. Moody, *Basic Deliverance Manual*

Derek Prince. *Fasting. God require His People To Humble Themselves Before Him And Has Revealed A Simple, Practical Way To Accomplish This.*

Lynn Hardy. *Destroying The Curses In The Court Of Heaven.*

Michael J. Norton (2011) *A Field Guide To Spiritual Warfare: The Power To Pull The Impossible From Heavenly The Realm.* Destiny Image, USA.

Derek Prince. (2003) *War in Heaven: God's Epic Battle With Evil.* Chosen Books, United State Of America.

Christ Embassy Healing School. 2020. *Faith Proclamation of Healing and Health Vol 2,*

Dr D.K Olukoya. *Prayer Rain: The Most Powerful and Practical Prayer Manual Ever Written,* MFM Ministry, Nigeria.

Christopher Monaghan. *The Power Of Worship.*

Mark Driscoll and DR Gerry Breshears, *Worship: God transforms.*

Don't miss out!

Visit the website below and you can sign up to receive emails whenever Johannes Tefo publishes a new book. There's no charge and no obligation.

https://books2read.com/r/B-A-UEZX-EAGBD

Connecting independent readers to independent writers.

Did you love *Generational Curses And Spiritual Warfare: Spiritual Strategies & Principles Of Victory Against Evil Strongholds*? Then you should read *Battle In The Sea: How To Tackle Spiritual Warfare And Win The Battle*[1] by Johannes Tefo!

[2]

This is a must-have book about how to tackle spiritual warfare and win in the name of the LORD. Through this profound book, you will come out armed with strategic prayers to silence the powers that have been harassing' and messing with your life. The marine kingdom is one of the deadliest kingdoms of Satan, located under the sea. This book came through a revelation. As someone who has been the victim of evil, as we all are, the LORD has been gracious to me, teaching my hands how to wage the right warfare against the enemy.Through years of experience and the work of the Holy Spirit, this is the book to amplify your inner

---

1. https://books2read.com/u/49aE5X

2. https://books2read.com/u/49aE5X

man and strengthen you in times like this. Believers have to take territory, win souls, and deliver captives, this is a must-have book filled with wisdom and knowledge for your spiritual deliverance.

Also by Johannes Tefo

Family spiritual Warfare Books
Generational Curses And Spiritual Warfare: Spiritual Strategies &
Principles Of Victory Against Evil Strongholds
Youth's Guide To Spiritual Warfare
A Women's Guide To Spiritual Warfare

Standalone
Deliver Your Soul From Evil
Overcoming Spirit Of Stagnation
The 24: Prophetic Word For This Season 2024 And Beyond
Michael For Warfare
Territorial Spirits: Overcome Evil Strongholds in Your Life And Take
Over Your Community With Strategic Warfare And Winning Prayers
Prayers Against Suicide Spirit
Spiritual Warfare When Enough is Enough
Identity In Christ
Prayers Against Satanic Networks
The Workplace You Need: Spiritual Warfare Prayers That Silence Evil
Powers At Your Workplace.
Deliverance From Mind Control: Be Free And Delivered From Every
Marine Demons Of Mind Control
Times Getting Hard: Scriptures Of Comfort For Hard Days

Battle In The Sea: How To Tackle Spiritual Warfare And Win The Battle

About the Author

Before he started writing Christian books, Johannes got a graduate degree in Film and Television from university of Johannesburg. After that, just to shake things up, he went to equip himself with religious studies, particularly Christianity, just to have knack about the world beyond the curtains of time. And how this body of Christ has transformed millions of people around the world, not neglecting how sadly the movement has been persecuted from time to time. He now writes full time.